CONTENTS

INTRODUCTION

A baseball bounces off an outfielder's head into the stands for a home run...

A basketball player barks like a dog while his opponents stare at him, astounded, and a teammate easily scores the winning basket...

A star football player recovers a fumble and races the length of the field—the wrong way...

Hockey fans celebrate goals by throwing octopuses on the ice...

For most of us, part of the fun of watching sports comes from the wild and wacky things that sometimes happen. What follows are dozens of offbeat anecdotes—odd-but-true sports stories that have amazed and amused fans for generations.

We hope you enjoy them, too!

CHAPTER

1

NOT FAIR

*There's a story told that before
ballparks had lights, during one late
inning of a baseball game, it was getting too dark for anyone to see what
was going on.*

*The pitcher pretended to throw
the ball, the catcher smacked his mitt
as if he'd caught the pitch, the umpire
called it a strike, and the batter
protested that it should have been
called a ball. But the pitch, of course,
was never thrown!*

*It's not known for sure that this
ever happened, but it certainly could
have. Sometimes in their eagerness to
win, players and their managers or
coaches take every opportunity to gain
an edge over their opponents.*

A Basketball Team's Best Friend

Surprise plays come when you *leash* expect them. And sometimes—as in the January 14, 1994, junior varsity high school basketball game between Casper, Wyoming, cross-town rivals, Natrona County and Kelly Walsh—they're a howling success.

Here's the tale (or should we say tail?): With the score tied at 63–all, just seconds remained in the game. A timeout had been called, and when play resumed Natrona would inbound the ball. As Natrona coach Tim Nolan was drawing up a standard play, someone in the team huddle offered a suggestion: "The Barking Dog!"

Teammates enthusiastically endorsed the idea, and, although later the coach didn't remember with certainty having given the go-ahead, he apparently went along with popular demand.

As Natrona was about to inbound the ball, the player who had volunteered for the part, Jason Holt, got down on all fours and began barking like a dog. Just about everyone, particularly the Kelly Walsh players, focused their attention on Jason, trying to figure out what was going on.

They learned soon enough. With the Kelly Walsh players' attention diverted and all eyes on Jason, Natrona inbounded the ball to Mike Hobart, who scored the uncontested basket that put his team ahead to stay, 65–63.

The play left some observers mutt-ering. They felt the "barking dog" play—which got national attention, including exposure on *The Tonight Show with Jay Leno*, was unsportsmanlike. But coach Nolan and the school's athletic director Glen Legler believe "kids should have fun" in their sports—and the play certainly was that.

Mash Appeal

"I was only trying to put some fun in the game," Dave Bresnahan claimed about a little trick he pulled the night of August 31, 1987.

A second-string catcher, he was behind the plate for the Cleveland Indians farm club, the Williamsport (Pa.) Bills of the Class AA Eastern League, as they faced Reading.

When Reading got a runner to third, Bresnahan called time and went to his bench, seemingly to get a new mitt. But what he really went back for was a potato he had peeled earlier.

Then, when he caught the next pitch, he switched the potato for the ball, and, in what appeared to be his attempt to pick the runner off third base, he threw it so that it "spud" past the sack. The runner, seeing the potato head for the outfield, and thinking it was the ball, dashed for home, only to find Dave waiting to tag him out with the actual ball.

The umpire, realizing that it was not a ball retrieved by the outfielder, was not amused and ruled the runner safe. Bresnahan protested that the rule book didn't say anything against throwing a potato in a game. But the ump stuck with his decision.

Not only that, but Dave's manager, Orlando Gomez, chipped in by taking the agi-tater out of the game and fining him fifty dollars. And, if that wasn't enough to take the starch out of him, the Indians dropped him like, well, a hot potato. His release by the Indians effectively mashed his hopes of a baseball career.

While some found the stunt appalling, many found it quite a-peeling. The next season, "The Potato Guy," as some called him, was honored by having his uniform retired at Williamsport. The ceremony was part of a promotion in which any fan with a potato could get into the game for a dollar. The night was a sellout and a (s)mash hit.

Even a decade later, his mail included a potato or two, sent to him by fans who asked that he autograph the tubers and mail them back in the enclosed envelopes.

Snow Problem

Snow fair, you say?

Late in the fourth quarter of a December 1982, football game, the awful weather conditions at Schaefer Field in Foxboro,

Massachusetts, had helped keep the home-team New England Patriots and visiting Miami Dolphins from scoring. Snow was falling, the wind was gusting up to thirty miles an hour, the temperature was twenty degrees, and neither team could mount much offense.

In the final period, the Patriots used eleven running plays to move the ball from their own seven-yard line into field-goal range. The kicker was soccer-style kicker John Smith, who had missed an eighteen-yard attempt in the second quarter due to the slippery conditions.

Now the Patriots called time out. On instructions from Patriots Coach Ron Meyer, a grounds crew member named Mark Henderson drove onto the field in a tractor with a plow attached. He proceeded to clear a small, narrow path on the snow-covered turf for Smith.

With the benefit of having a clear patch of turf for the kick, Smith converted the thirty-three-yard attempt with less than five minutes left in the game. The field goal was the only score in the game; the Patriots' 3–0 lead held up to be the final score.

Patriot fans hailed the plowing, but Dolphins coach Don Shula complained. "The officials shouldn't have let it happen.

The official nearest me didn't see the guy come out before it was too late. But we have no recourse, so let's forget it. I don't plan a protest." He must have figured it was *snow* use arguing.

Referee Bob Frederick contended, "Game officials have no control over the removal of the snow done by a maintenance man with a power brush on the plow."

Patriots coach Meyer said, "I would have waved the guy on the field for the Dolphins in a similar situation. It was just something that happened."

For his part, Henderson, a member of the maintenance crew, was delighted, too. There was even talk of giving him the game ball. It was enough that the crowd was chanting "MVP, MVP, MVP" for Henderson, a guy who wasn't ever officially in the game, but may well have been its most valuable participant.

Midget Baseball

The strike zone in baseball depends on the umpire's judgment and the size of the batter.

Since a large strike zone obviously favors

a pitcher and a small one favors the batter, what could be better than a midget-sized strike zone? It would practically guarantee that the batter would reach base with a walk. And who's more likely to have a midget-sized zone than a midget?

This had to be the thinking of owner Bill Veeck (rhymes with wreck) when he masterminded a once-in-a-lifetime event: sending up a midget to pinch-hit in a St. Louis Browns game. Eddie Gaedel, whose height barely reached 3'7", was put up to bat for Browns outfielder Frank Saucier, in the nightcap of a twin bill August 19, 1951. A fraction the size of the average player, he wore a Browns uniform with the number 1/8.

Gaedel's mission was just to stand there and draw a walk, a likely possibility in view of the tiny strike zone his short stature required.

When plate umpire Ed Hurley questioned his eligibility, Gaedel trotted to the dugout and returned with the ($100) contract he had signed. Then he stood with the bat on his shoulders while Tiger pitcher Bob Cain threw four straight balls, walking him. A pinch runner, Jim Delsing, then replaced Gaedel. The Browns won, 5–1.

But Gaedel's playing career was cut short. Citing the "best interests of baseball,"

Will Harridge, president of the American League, refused to approve the contract, thus ending Gaedel's one at-bat career.

Who's Got the Ball?

Coach Pop Warner of the Carlisle Indian Industrial School football team had pads sewn on the sleeves of his players' uniforms. Innocent enough, except that, when a player crossed his arms at the chest, the pads resembled a football.

This, of course, made it very difficult for opponents to figure out which Carlisle player was actually carrying the football. The trick helped Carlisle win a 1908 game against Syracuse University, 12–0.

But when Warner planned to use the technique against Harvard, Percy Haughter, the Harvard coach, said: "Pop, I realize the rules permit elbow pads, but the rules also state that the home team can choose the ball. Unless you remove those pads, I'll paint the ball red, white, and blue."

Since the trick would surely fail with a red, white, and blue ball, Pop had the pads removed. Sew much for that tricky strategy!

Who's Got the Ball? Part II

When they weren't giving the appearance of carrying a football, the Carlisle players had other tricks up their sleeves—-or elsewhere on their uniforms.

Once, in another game against Harvard, the Carlisle quarterback took the ball from center and shoved it under the back of the jersey of teammate Charlie Dillon. The fooled Harvard players chased the quarterback, while Dillon easily scored a touchdown. (The next year, the Rules Committee outlawed the trick.)

Carlisle wasn't the only team to employ this ruse. In a play in an 1895 game against Vanderbilt University, Auburn University's coach John Heisman (for whom the trophy for best college player is named) had his quarterback hide the football under *his* jersey. The quarterback was able to run fifty yards for a touchdown, while Vanderbilt players tried in vain to determine who had the ball.

CHAPTER
2

FAN-ATICS

Fans help make sports what they are. They can be wise, wild, funny, and sometimes outrageous. No wonder the word "fans" is short for "fanatic."

Team owners, of course, depend on fans, and will go to great lengths to attract spectators to a game.

Fans Managed OK

"Boy, if I were the manager..."

How many baseball fans have said that!

The late Bill Veeck, owner of the St. Louis Browns, understood the feeling, and capitalized on it.

Veeck tried various innovations to entertain fans. He gave orchids to women, put gift certificates beneath seats, introduced exploding scoreboards, set up an outdoor shower head for bleacher fans, and even had circus clowns in the coaching boxes.

He offered all sorts of inducements to encourage more people to attend St. Louis Browns games. Once, the story goes, someone he urged to come to a game asked, "What time does it start?"

"What time's convenient?" Veeck replied.

On August 25, 1951, he established Grandstand Managers Day and let about a thousand fans set the lineup and game strategy for the Browns. Team representatives would hold up large signs asking such questions as "Infield In?" and "Should we walk him?" and 1,115 customers in the stands would indicate what to do by showing lettered "yes" or "no" signs they'd been given. Circuit Judge James E. McLaughlin tabulated the fans' votes.

The Browns' lineup, determined by the fans, included two recently benched players —catcher Sherm Lollar and first baseman Hank Arft. Rewarding the fans' confidence, each drove in two runs, Lollar with a homer, double and single. He also scored three runs.

Veeck also wanted to use two fans as coaches on the baseline, but the American League wouldn't approve the contracts. So, the honorary coaches were seated near the Browns dugout in a box, along with the Browns' manager, Zack Taylor, who reclined in a rocking chair. The fan-coaches communicated with Coach John Bernardino by walkie-talkie.

The first question put to the grandstand managers came in the bottom of the first, after Gus Zernial put the Athletics ahead with a three-run homer. His teammate, Pete Suder, came up to bat with men on first and third, and the fans were asked whether the Browns infield should play in to try to cut off a run, or play back and try for a double play. The fans voted for the infield to stay back, and, sure enough, Suder batted into a double play.

Then in the Browns' half of the first, with Lollar on first, one out and the count 3–2 on Cliff Mapes, the majority voted against having Lollar break for second on the next pitch. Their decision proved correct when Mapes struck out.

They were wrong on one decision after the Browns tied the score in the first. With two out and Arft on first after a single, the grandstand managers voted for him to steal, and he was pegged out by a couple of feet.

Jimmy Dykes, manager of the opposing team, the Philadelphia Athletics, had threatened to ask that the game be forfeited if the grandstand managing tactics delayed the game too much. But the game took only two hours eleven minutes.

Grandstand managing, which Veeck called "our great experiment," was offered only in that one game, but it worked, as the last-place Browns beat the Philadelphia Athletics, 5–3, and improved their record to 38–81, only 38 1/2 games out of first place!

War Games

During the Civil War, baseball was already so popular that during quiet periods along the front, truces were sometimes arranged for North–South games to be played.

A Dog-gone Great Day

It was a bone-a-fido offer.

On August 28, 1996, all dogs accompanied by their owner got into the Chicago White Sox ballgame free at Comiskey Park.

There were 321 four-legged fans and 17,269 two-legged ones at the game. The club provided a grass patch with hydrants for the dogs to use and Frisbees for them to catch, and sponsored a "Best-Dressed Dog" contest.

In August 1999, the annual Dog Days of August promotion by the Chicago White Sox attracted over 500 canines.

Rally 'Round the Flag (pole)

Fan support of a team reached new heights on May 31, 1949, when a diehard Cleveland Indians rooter, retailer Charles Lupica, climbed a 65-foot flagpole at his store. He vowed not to come back down until the Indians were back in first place where they had finished the season before.

Lupica's devotion never flagged. For 117 days straight—even when his wife gave birth to their son on August 7—he lived on the flagpole on a 4' by 6' platform. On September 25, the flagpole and Charles were brought to Cleveland Stadium where he was brought down, ending his streak of almost four months aloft.

While the Indians never got to first place that season, it was a banner year for their star fan. Lupica certainly earned his stripes, and deserves a salute.

Free Agent Fan

Major league baseball lets players become "free agents" and shop around among teams for the best deal they can get. Also, ball clubs frequently trade away veteran players. As a result, rosters are constantly changing, and some fans find it difficult to keep rooting for the same team.

Michael Volpe had been supporting the San Francisco Giants for thirty-six years. But in November 1996, when the Giants traded his favorite player, Matt Williams, to the Cleveland Indians, Volpe got angry and decided to become a "free agent fan."

The forty-five-year-old business consultant wrote letters to 27 other Major League teams, asking "Why should I become a fan of your team?" He got answers from twenty-three clubs.

After evaluating his "fan mail," he decided he'd root for the Philadelphia Phillies and the minor league Durham Bulls.

Lots—and Lots!—of Luck

Fans will go to any lengths to let their favorite athletes know how they feel about them.

Need proof? Well, in March 1965 Princeton students sent a six-word good-luck telegram to their basketball team in Portland, Oregon, where the Tigers were going to meet Michigan in an NCAA semi-final game.

Nothing unusual about the telegram, except that the $240 worth of greetings also carried more than 2,000 signatures, bringing the word count to over 4,000! One of the longest non-diplomatic telegrams ever, it extended more than 200 feet, over twice the length of a standard basketball court!

Hats Off!

You've got to take your hat off to any player who scores three goals in a single hockey game.

As a matter of fact, that rare feat has come to be known as "the hat trick." Why? Because in the late 1930s, a haberdasher in Toronto began giving a hat to any Toronto hockey player who accomplished the feat. Then, in the 1940s, fans started the custom of throwing hats on the ice when a player scored his third goal of the game.

A "pure" or "natural" hat trick—very, very rare—is the term for a player scoring three consecutive goals in a game without anyone else scoring in between.

Icing the Octopus

Beginning in the 1950s, Detroit Red Wing fans had a different way of showing their appreciation for the home team—they threw octopuses onto the ice for good luck.

The icing-the-octopus fad had its origins in 1952, when Pete Cusimano and his late brother, Jerry, who both worked in their family's seafood business, were rooting for the Red Wings to win eight straight playoff games. At the time, a team had to win just four games in the first round and four in the second to become the Stanley Cup champions. The Red Wings had just eliminated the Toronto Maple Leafs in four straight and, now skating against the Montreal Canadiens, were on their way to a sweep.

Jerry picked up an octopus and, pointing out that it had eight arms, representing eight wins, suggested throwing it on the ice as a good-luck omen. That weekend, after the Detroit team had scored its first goal, Pete threw the octopus. A linesman skated over to pick it up but, thinking the slimy, wiggling, Jell-O-like creature was alive, drew back. The public address announcer proclaimed, "Octopi shall not occupy the ice. Please refrain from throwing same."

(The Cusimanos' octopus was boiled, giving it a red-wine glow, in contrast with the live octopuses other fans have thrown since.)

The brothers had planned to hurl an octopus just once, but, after the Red Wings won the game 3-0 and went on to win the Stanley Cup in eight straight games, they decided to try again the next year.

The good-luck charm didn't work that season, as the Wings were upset in the 1953 semi-finals by Boston, but it did work two more seasons after that. And Pete kept the tradition alive. The octopus-throwing custom spread, even to fans of other teams, and one eight-armed critter was even thrown during the 1994 Olympics.

A Michigan fish company, billing itself as the "O-Fish-Al" playoff octopus supplier, was selling an Octo-Kit, complete with a cooked octopus, two latex gloves, and two wet-naps in a sealed plastic bag.

By 1995, the Red Wings and other teams were urging fans to deposit their octopuses in boxes rather than throw them on the ice, because the practice delays the game and hurts momentum after a home-team goal. In April 1997, the Red Wings and Joe Louis Arena officials said that octopuses would not be allowed into the building for any of the Red Wings home playoff games.

The *Rat* Trick

In Ft. Lauderdale, Florida, at the first 1995–96 season home game of the Florida Panthers, Scott Mellanby of the Panthers swatted a rat running across the locker room with his stick, ending its career. Scott then went out and scored two goals, an accomplishment that teammate, goalie John Vanbiesbrouck, labeled a *"rat* trick."

Learning what had happened, fans began bringing plastic or rubber rats to games at the Miami Arena (which someone referred to as the "Rat's Nest") and throwing them on the ice after a Panther goal. Soon the practice exploded into a full-fledged fad. Some fans dressed their rubber rats in sweaters and some painted messages to players on them.

But then the National Hockey League officially frowned on throwing real octopuses or make-believe rats. In the 1996–97 season, the NHL threatened home teams with first a warning, then a two-minute delay-of-game penalty for any such creatures thrown by home fans onto the rink.

Rats.

Out of This World

Fans of the Cleveland Browns couldn't wait until a professional football team with that name returned to Cleveland, after losing their beloved franchise for economic reasons.

In April 1997, astronaut Dr. Donald R. Thomas, a diehard Cleveland Browns fan, was among the crew members on a mission aboard the space shuttle *Columbia*.

He wore a Browns patch on his space suit, carried a Browns team flag and wore a Browns watch. The watch ticked off the days until August 21, 1999, when National Football League commissioner Paul Tagliabue promised that a franchise called the Browns would play in a new Cleveland Browns Stadium.

Wrong Number

Mark Landsberger, who played basketball for Chicago, L.A., and Atlanta in the late '70s and early '80s, was giving his autograph to a young fan, who asked, "Can you put your number down?" The fan meant his uniform number, but Mark wrote down his unlisted phone number.

Hair's to Bryant

Bryant Reeves, center for the Vancouver Grizzlies in the National Basketball Association, is a very popular athlete. Just ask the two thousand-plus fans to whom he gave free tickets in 1995 for shaving their head in the buzz cut style worn by Reeves.

CHAPTER

3

BRING IN THE CLOWNS

Much of the fun provided by professional sports is produced by the amusing characters the games attract.

Grapefruit League

Among the funniest men who ever donned a big-league baseball uniform was Charles Dillon Stengel, nicknamed "Casey" for K.C., the abbreviation of Kansas City, his hometown. Casey was a player, coach or manager on seventeen professional baseball teams, including four New York clubs, the Yankees, Giants, Dodgers, and Mets.

Because many Major League baseball teams do their spring training in warm-weather areas where citrus fruits thrive, pre-season competition there has come to be known as "the grapefruit league." You might consider it pulp fiction, but in 1915 Casey was involved in one of the juiciest "grapefruit league" incidents ever.

The victim of the prank was Casey's manager, Wilbert "Uncle Robbie" Robinson, who was quite a character himself. Robinson once started a Bonehead Club for stupid plays, and then became its first member when he handed the plate umpire the wrong line-up card. And once he kept a player out of the line-up because he couldn't spell the player's name!

According to one popular version, after a ballplayer, Gabby Street, had caught a baseball dropped from the Washington

Monument, Casey wondered whether a man could catch a baseball dropped from an airplane. Ruth Law, a pioneer woman aviator, agreed to fly a plane over the Dodgers' training grounds in Daytona Beach, Florida, from which a baseball, supposedly supplied by Stengel, would be dropped.

By time of the drop, though, the baseball had been replaced by a grapefruit. When the pilot dropped it, Robinson, the manager of the Dodgers, camped under what he thought was a baseball. The manager, who'd been warming up a pitcher, waved everyone else away in the style of an outfielder, yelling, "I've got it, I've got it."

He got it, all right. The grapefruit landed smack on his glove, and fragments of the fruit flew everywhere, leaving seeds on his uniform and face, with a force that made Uncle Robbie fear he'd been mortally wounded. The impact knocked him on his back. Players came running up to their fallen manager, who apparently was all right, and everyone started laughing—except Robinson. For him, it was the pits.

A Colorful Character

Charlie Kerfeld, a relief pitcher for the Houston Astros for a brief time in the 1980s, once had lightning bolts shaved into the side of his hair (and painted them green for St. Patrick's Day).

But his bizarre ideas were not exclusive to his hairstyles. He once settled a contract dispute with the Astros when the club agreed to give him thirty-seven boxes of Jell-O. He made two demands about the Jell-O:

- It had to be orange because the team had decided to abandon its wildly colored uniforms, and
- There had to be thirty-seven boxes of the dessert because thirty-seven had been the number worn by some of baseball's great characters.

Charlie was a colorful character himself.

Tattooed Traffic Stopper

Speaking of characters, there's truly none more colorful—literally—than the NBA's leading rebounder five years in a row (1992–1996), Dennis Rodman. An often outrageous personality, he's known for turning heads with stunts like frequently changing the color of his hair or wearing a wedding dress to an autograph signing for his first book, *Bad As I Wanna Be*.

When he played for San Antonio, Dennis decided to bleach his hair blond. (The beauty treatment made him thirty minutes late for the dedication to the new arena, the

Alamodome.) As time went on, he'd dye his close-cut hair red or orange, fuchsia, green or mellow yellow, depending on his mood, During the 1995 playoffs, as a member of the Chicago Bulls, he had a red AIDS ribbon colored into the back of his green hair.

A Chicago department store, Bigsby & Kruthers, had Dennis's portrait painted on the side of its building along the Kennedy Expressway in March 1996. The addition of Rodman's picture on the store's 32' x 75' mural caused quite a stir, evoking mixed reactions from the public. One change in hair color—from blonde to red—was made on the mural, just as Dennis had changed his actual hair. The store was prepared to make other color changes if Dennis dyed his hair again, but there was a problem: once Dennis's portrait went up, the mural stopped traffic, with motorists wanting to take photos or just gape at the controversial athlete. So, after a few weeks, Dennis' portrait was taken down.

His devil-may-care playing style has had some strange consequences. In his third year with the Detroit Pistons, in a game in the Silverdome, Dennis went diving wildly for a ball heading out of bounds and landed on a woman seated in the front row, knocking out some of her teeth. He paid about

$60,000 in dental bills.

When he first came to the Bulls from the Pistons, he couldn't have his old uniform number 10, because that was already being worn by Bob Love. So, he requested 91. Any uniform number over 55 requires league approval, which Rodman obtained. Why, besides wanting to be different, did Dennis want number 91? First, 9 and 1 add up to 10, his old number. And, he asked, "What are the first two numbers you dial in emergencies? Who do you call to put out the fire?"

New Pitch

After Barry Larkin of the Cincinnati Reds hit a home run off Bob Patterson, relief pitcher for the Chicago Cubs, Patterson described the pitch this way: "It was a cross between a screwball and a change-up. It was a screw-up."

4

WRONG WAYS, MISPLAYS

Even the best athletes have bad days, and unfortunately, some are remembered for the one bad play rather than all the good plays of their careers.

He Went That Way

You know how in Westerns, the marshal always does the right thing and rides the bad guys out of town? Well, here's one marshal(l) who thought he was doing the right thing, but did quite the opposite.

It happened in the fourth quarter of a National Football Game between the Minnesota Vikings and the San Francisco 49ers in October 1964, when the 49ers' Billy Kilmer caught a pass from George Mira, ran a few steps, and fumbled.

Jim Marshall, who enjoyed an outstanding career as Vikings defensive end, grabbed the ball on the run and took off with the recovered fumble. The Marshall Plan was to race for the goal line sixty-two yards away. Unfortunately, it was the *wrong* goal line!

As Marshall ran, his teammates both on and off the field frantically yelled and waved their arms to let him know he was going the wrong way. But Marshall thought they were cheering him on. And when his quarterback, Fran Tarkenton, ran along the sidelines and desperately pointed, Jim figured Fran was just urging him to run faster.

After Marshall crossed the goal line, the 49ers were awarded a 2-point safety. When

Jim realized the error of his ways, he hurled the football out of bounds. Luckily, he didn't just drop the ball to the ground in the end zone, or the 49ers could have pounced on it for a touchdown.

It wouldn't have done any good if Tarkenton or another teammate had tackled him during his wrong-way run. The tackler would have been thrown out of the game, the Vikings would have been penalized fifteen yards, and the 49ers might still have been awarded the safety if an official ruled that if not for the tackle, Jim would have crossed the goal line.

Fortunately, despite Marshall's goof, the Vikings won, 27–22.

Run for the Roses

Memorable wrong-way runs were nothing new in football. One of the most infamous took place in the 1929 Rose Bowl game between Georgia Tech and the University of California.

In the second quarter of a scoreless game, Roy Riegels, of California, snatched up a Georgia Tech fumble.

Hugging the pigskin, he cut back across

the field to evade tacklers. Then confusion set in, causing Roy to reverse direction. He raced down the sideline for the goal line, all right, but it was the *wrong* goal line.

When his teammate, halfback Benny Lom, realized what was happening, Lom charged after Riegels. Hearing footsteps behind him, Riegels did what any self-respecting ball-carrier being pursued would do: He just put on more speed. It wasn't until he'd run about sixty yards and was at the three-yard line that Lom grabbed him, just as a wave of Tech tacklers bowled-over Riegels, hurtling him to the one-yard line.

Spared from giving up a wrong-way touchdown, California immediately got into punt formation. Riegels nervously (as you would imagine) snapped the ball to Lom, who tried to get off a punt. But a Tech tackle broke through the line and blocked the kick, and the ball rolled out of the end zone. The officials ruled that it rolled out after being touched by a California player, and so they awarded Georgia Tech a safety.

The Roy-al foul-up may not have seemed too significant at the moment, but the two points awarded for the safety, the first score of the game, were enough to provide the difference between victory and defeat. Tech won, 8–7.

Rotten Cotton

In all team sports, the outcome of games is often decided by the players who come into the contest off the bench. That's one reason coaches want all their players, subs included, to stay ready for action. But sometimes a sub is so caught up in the play that he comes off the bench—uninvited and illegally.

An example of this took place in the 1955 Cotton Bowl game, when Dickie Moegle of Rice was running down the field and headed for a touchdown, when an Alabama player, Tommy Lewis, sitting on the bench, couldn't contain himself. Lewis leaped off the bench onto the playing field and tackled Moegle.

But the officials didn't condone Lewis' action, and his attempted bale-out didn't work. Rice was awarded the touchdown, because it was ruled that Moegle would have scored if he hadn't been crushed by Lewis' illegal tackle.

Reporting for Duty

In baseball back in the 1880s, the rules allowed a sub to enter the game just by reporting to the umpire.

Once, when a foul ball was hit out of the

reach of his team's catcher, King Kelly, captain of the Boston Braves, jumped up from the bench to catch it. As he was making the play, he yelled to the umpire: "Kelly now catching for Boston."

Mystery Basket

Sports officials are all-seeing and all-knowing—or are they?

In the 1951-52 NBA championship series, the New York Knicks faced the Minneapolis Lakers. In the first half of the first game, Al McGuire of the Knicks netted a jump shot and was fouled. He should have been awarded one free throw, but—what's this?—he was given two shots, as if he hadn't scored the basket. It seems everyone in the arena had seen the shot go in, except the two referees.

The Knicks coach, Joe Lapchick, and others went wild, but since the refs hadn't seen the shot go in, the basket could not count. Even the chief of referees,who was present at the game as an observer, could do nothing about the oversight.

McGuire made both foul shots, adding 2 points to the Knicks' score, rather than the

3 they would have had from McGuire's basket plus one foul shot. That one-point difference resulted in a tie game at the end of regulation time, rather than a Knick victory. The game was then won by the Lakers in overtime, 83–79. The Lakers went on to win the series, four games to three.

Give the refs an assist.

Foul Ball

Fan-friendly ballplayers will sometimes toss a ball to a spectator for a souvenir. But here's one souvenir the generous player would like to forget.

The Los Angeles Dodgers were playing the Montreal Expos at home during the 1994 season, and with one out and a man on first, Dodger Jose Offerman hit a ball to right that was caught by right-fielder Larry Walker for the second out.

But Walker, thinking it was the third out, flipped the ball to a fan in the stands and started jogging off the field as the base runner raced around the bases. Realizing his mistake, Walker got the ball back from the fan, and threw it to the plate, but not in time to prevent the runner from scoring.

Didn't Have a Prayer

When a coach scolds a player for failing to do his job, the player better have a good excuse. Here's one that's tough to beat...

In a 1933 pro football game between the New York Giants and Chicago Bears, Ken Strong, the Giants' great place kicker, connected on a field goal, but the play was called back. The same thing happened again, and once more Strong had to try. This time, his kick was good, the Giants stayed onsides, and the three points counted.

On each of Strong's attempts, the Giants coach Steve Owen noticed that Joe Kopcha, a guard for the Bears, had been on his knees, but that Owen's brother, Bill, a 250-pound Giant player, hadn't tried to block Kopcha. The coach angrily summoned Bill to the sidelines. "What was the matter with you?" he demanded. "You had Kopcha set up for a clean shot at him and you never touched him."

"I just couldn't do it, Steve," Bill said. "Every time Ken got ready to kick, Kopcha dropped on his knees and said, 'Please, God, don't let him make it.' And, gosh, Steve, I couldn't smack a man when he's praying, could I?"

The coach just smiled and walked away.

Short Walk

One suggestion to speed-up baseball games is to have three balls, not four, constitute a walk. At least one time, that happened without a rule change, and it was costly.

In the third inning of a game in Toronto on July 22, 1995, the Cleveland Indians had two baserunners on and two men out. The count on the batter, Jim Thome, went to 2-2. The next pitch was a ball. It should have brought the count to 3-2, but the plate umpire mistakenly thought the pitch was ball four. Apparently, none of the other umpires and no one on the Toronto Blue Jays realized the mistake, and no one complained.

The mistaken ball-four call resulted in loaded bases, and the next batter cleared them with a triple. The Indians walked away with the game, 4–2.

Lucky Bounce

There are times when a basketball seems to have a mind of its own, and there's not much a defender can do about it, when, say, the ball bounces off an opposing player's head for a score (which has happened). But what about times when there was something the defender *could* have done, but didn't?

Take, for instance, the February 5, 1965, game between the New York Knicks and Detroit Pistons, which was down to its final seconds, with the Pistons leading by 2, 108–106. In desperation, Tom Gola of the Knicks grabbed a Piston pass near the Detroit goal as he was falling out of bounds. And, to prevent the ball from going out of bounds, hurled it way down court, toward the Knick basket.

The only player in the far court was the Pistons' Terry Dischinger. Apparently, because he was aware that time was running out and since there wasn't a Knick in sight, he made no attempt to catch the ball.

It made sense, right? Wrong! It turned out to be a big mistake. The ball bounced once near the foul line and went right into the basket, tying the score at 108 and forcing the game into overtime. The Knicks, who'd been a heartbeat away from a loss, went on to win the game, 118–112.

For New York, the lucky bounce happened in the Knick of time.

Unhappy Hat Trick

As proud an achievement as a hat trick is, you can understand why Paul Coffey of the Detroit Red Wings would have preferred to skip the honor in the first game of the Western Conference Playoff against the Colorado Avalanche, in May 1996.

Paul scored both his team's goals that night—but he also scored one for the Avalanche.

Forty-four seconds into the second period, two Avalanche skaters broke away for a two-on-one rush. As Red Wing goalie Chris Osgood came out of the net, Stephan Yelle of

Colorado skated in, then passed the puck back into the slot, and onto Coffey's stick.

Apparently forgetting the direction of the play or which end of the rink the Wings were defending, Coffey fired into the net— the wrong one.

The goal was critical, as the Avalanche went on to win the game, 3–2 (and the series, 4 games to 2). A Red Wing fan threw a hat onto the rink, in sarcastic tribute to Coffey's unorthodox hat trick.

Shaved by the Bell

Abbes Tehami was first across the finish line at the 1991 Brussels Marathon in Belgium. But oddly, he didn't have the mustache he'd had at the start of the race.

The mystery was solved when it was discovered that the mustached man who started the race wasn't Abbes but his coach, who ran the early miles in his place, then passed his number to Tehami, who ran the last part of the race.

Needless to say, Tehami's clever ruse disqualified him from winning the event.

CHAPTER
5

LOVABLE LOSERS

Sports history is populated by "lovable losers"—teams and individual athletes who perform poorly, but who, because of a combination of personality and effort, are adored by the fans.

The expansion team of the early 1960s, the New York Mets, are a prime example. Despite a dreadful losing record (40–120) their first year, they drew nearly a million fans.

Marvelous...Not!

One of the Mets most beloved players was first baseman Marv Throneberry, a slugger who was sarcastically nicknamed "Marvelous Marv" for his fielding ineptness. Though Marv had many bad days as a Met, perhaps none was worse than June 17, 1962, when the Mets lost a double-header to the Chicago Cubs.

In the first inning when the Cubs leadoff hitter Don Landrum was caught in a rundown, Marv blocked the basepath. This error let the runner go to second, and opened the floodgates for a four-run inning that would have been scoreless if not for the misplay. So, thanks to Marv's mishap, the Cubs scored four unearned runs.

In the bottom of the first, the Mets scored a run and had two runners on base, when Throneberry belted a base hit deep to right field and, glad to have avenged his misplay, stopped at third. But he was called out for failing to touch first base. Casey Stengel, the Mets manager, came out to protest, but an umpire told Casey not to bother—"He missed second base, too."

In the bottom of the ninth the Mets rallied to trail only by 8–7. There was a runner on first, and Marv was up with another chance to redeem himself. But he struck out swinging.

In general, it was his fielding that got most of the negative attention. In fact once on Marv's birthday, manager Casey Stengel said he would have given Marv a piece of birthday cake, but was afraid he'd drop it.

Eddie the Eagle

Few losers in sports history have been as beloved as Eddie "the Eagle" Edwards, whose misfortunes would have grounded a lesser bird.

At the time of the 1988 Winter Olympic Games in Calgary, Canada, Eddie had been ski-jumping for only two years. But the 5'8" English construction worker, who wore glasses with lenses so thick he could hardly see the landing zone, was determined to compete in the Olympics.

When he first tried ski jumping at Lake Placid, New York, he wore a helmet held around his neck by string. His borrowed boots were so big he had to wear six pairs of sox to fit in them.

Eddie had universal appeal. Once, his old helmet came off when he was in midair, and

Italian skiers bought him a new one.
Austrians bought him new skis, and West
Germans provided him with a ski outfit.
Eddie was also invited to train with the
Norwegian, Finnish, German, and United
States teams.

Eddie was willing to suffer for his ambition. While training in Finland, he lived "on bread and jam" in a mental institution because it cost only one pound a night. Eddie was a part-time plasterer who did odd jobs such as snow-shoveling and baby-sitting to help pay for his skiing. Once, when he suffered a broken jaw, he tied a scarf around it and continued competing, because he couldn't afford medical treatment.

When he arrived in Calgary for the Olympics, he was greeted by a banner: *Welcome Eddie the Eagle Edwards.*

The fates were not so welcoming. His ski bindings were crushed in his luggage; on the first day of training jumps, he missed two jumps because he was locked out of the waxing hut, and after one practice jump, on which he did poorly, he was locked out of the cabin where his credentials were. Finally, Austrian skiers gave him a lift to the Olympic Village. ("I got lost there, too," he told an interviewer.)

Still, he was prepared to compete at Calgary in the seventy-meter and ninety-meter jumps. "I can jump as far as anyone," he said, "if I can stand it. I usually begin to get nervous when I've been up there past eighty meters."

He used to get "very scared" at the top of a jump, he said, "thinking of a million reasons not to go down there. You have to fight the fear that your next jump could be your last." Eddie, who started ski-jumping on a class trip when he was eleven, said that just before he jumped in the Olympics, he would hold a lucky gold boot his girlfriend had given him and say to himself, "May I survive."

At the 1988 Winter Olympic Games, Eddie was still the crowd favorite. Unfortunately, Eddie finished last in both the seventy-meter and ninety-meter jumps. There was some consolation, however. In the ninty-meter, even though he jumped only seventy-one meters, it was three meters better than the best by a Briton to that point. Accordingly, a London newspaper reported: "EDDIE SURVIVES AND BREAKS BRITISH RECORD."

At Last, A Happy Ending

All bad things—like good things—come to an end, eventually.

The Rutgers-Camden Pioneers and their fans knew it was only a matter of time. And, sure enough, on January 7, 1997, at their home gym in Camden, New Jersey, the basketball team beat Bloomfield College,

77–72, ending a 117-game losing streak, the longest in college basketball history.

Actually, the Rutgers-Camden streak needn't have been that long. The Pioneers could have won a game in the 1994–95 season on a technicality, when the New Jersey Athletic Conference ruled that Rowan College used an ineligible player and would have to forfeit its 85-56 victory.

But Wilbur "Pony" Wilson, who was then the Rutgers-Camden coach, turned down the "gift," saying, "I'd rather beat a team on the court," and the winless streak continued.

After the end of the losing streak, freshman Dawan Boxley said, "We're only a trivia question now.... We're on a one-game winning streak."

Save the Pigskin

The Chicago Bears demolished the Washington Redskins 73–0 in the National League Championship game on December 6, 1940. The score could have been even more lopsided, but the Bears stopped kicking extra points in the second half. The reason: In those days, fans were allowed to keep balls kicked into the stands, and

Washington, the home team, was afraid it would run out of footballs if the Bears kept kicking extra points!

Out on a Walk

After an out with nobody on base, infielders usually throw the ball to one another—sometimes with interesting results.

In 1966, when Orlando Cepeda was with the St. Louis Cardinals, and playing against his old teammates, the San Francisco Giants, the count on him was 3–2. Juan Marichal threw what he thought was called strike three. So did the catcher, Tom Haller, who threw the ball to the third baseman, who started throwing the ball around the infield.

But the umpire had called it ball four, and the Giants angrily surrounded the ump, yelling at him. Cepeda realized nobody had called time out, so after touching first base, he kept running and came into second standing up—only to find the Giants' second baseman, Hal Lanier, holding the ball that was being thrown around the infield.

So he was out at second on a walk.

Good News, Bad News

"Always a bridesmaid, never a bride" is a term given to people who never quite make it to the top spot. You could apply it to actors and actresses often nominated for an Academy Award who haven't won an Oscar...and to the Buffalo Bills.

The Bills were good enough to accomplish the remarkable feat of playing in the Super Bowl four years in a row, but not good enough to win any of them. From 1990 through 1993, the Bills lost all four Super Bowl games they played.

Doubly Bad

In 1975, Joe Torre (who years later would manage the New York Yankees to several baseball world championships) was a hard-hitting all-star player. That year, he set a National League record (and tied an American League mark) for double plays in a nine-inning game...as a batter!

Playing for the New York Mets, he hit into four double plays in a single game! The former MVP doesn't take all the credit himself —"You need a Felix Millan to go four for four ahead of you and have fewer than two outs when you come up to bat with him on base."

At least two of the double-play grounders were hard-hit balls, Torre says, but right at infielders. "There's no way to avoid hitting into a double play," he comments. "If you deliberately try to keep it from happening, you're likely to try to do things unnaturally, and you'll handicap yourself so that you don't hit solidly."

On one of the balls, hit right at the short-stop, he realized he'd mistakenly been trying to pull the ball. So the next time, he just hit the ball hard—right to the second baseman.

Stop Sign

Speaking the same language is not a guarantee of good communication.

One time, as Bud Harrelson of the New York Mets was rounding third base, the third-base coach Eddie Yost, yelled, "Whoa, whoa." But Harrelson went right by him and was thrown out at at home.

When Yost later asked Harrelson, "Why didn't you stop? I was yelling 'Whoa,'" Bud replied, "I thought you said, 'Go.'"

6

HELP FROM
A FRIEND

*Sometimes, help comes to athletes
from the most unexpected sources,
human and otherwise. For instance...*

Shoe Polish

The so-called "Miracle" team, the 1969 New York Mets, led the Baltimore Orioles in the World Series three games to one.

In the fifth game, played October 16, 1969, the Orioles had a 3–0 lead in the top of the sixth inning. Slugger Frank Robinson claimed he'd been hit on the right hip by a pitch, but plate umpire Lou DiMuro ruled that the ball had bounced off his bat first and was therefore a strike. Robinson proceeded to strike out.

In the bottom of the sixth, Cleon Jones led off for the Mets and was struck on the instep of his right foot by a dropping curveball that bounded into the Mets dugout. At first, the umpire called the pitch a ball, but Jones insisted the pitch had struck him. The Mets manager, Gil Hodges, showed a ball to the umpire, who saw that it had a tiny shoepolish smudge on it. He reversed his call and waved Jones to first base.

Cleon scored when Donn Clendenon followed with his third home run of the Series, bringing the Mets to within one run of the Orioles. The Mets won the game, 5–3, and the Series, four games to one.

Was the smudged ball that Hodges threw to the umpire the one that had supposedly hit Jones? It's not certain. Casey Stengel, the wily jokester who had managed the Mets in their "lovable loser" days, said, "Always keep some balls with polish on them around the dugout."

Snapshot

In game three of the first-round 1996–97 NHL playoffs between the New York Rangers and the Florida Panthers, Esa Tikkanen of the Rangers thought he had scored the winning goal on a slap shot that flew out of the goal.

At first the shot was disallowed. But the puck had hit a tiny camera mounted on the top of a post high *inside* the net. And when the replay official studied the shot from various angles, he saw that the camera had been jarred. Also, the noise the puck made — a "clunk" rather than the usual "ping" sound that a puck hitting a crossbar would make — indicated it had hit the camera.

The snap-shot gave the Rangers a 4–3 overtime victory.

Tale of the Tape

It's a definite no-no for a student to write the answers to a quiz on his hand or shirt-sleeve. But, as far we know, there's no such rule in football.

In December 1965, the Baltimore Colts were in contention for the playoffs, but their star quarterback, Johnny Unitas, and number-one backup, Gary Cuozzo, were injured. So when the team came to play the Rams in Los Angeles, the Colts turned to Tom Matte and Ed Brown. Matte, who had played several pro football seasons as a halfback, had played quarterback at Ohio State University.

"I didn't have time to get scared," he later recalled. "I also didn't have time to prepare because I came down with the flu that week and had to jam everything into the last couple of days. I had all our plays written on adhesive tape around my wrist, a crib sheet of sorts.

"With me in there at quarterback, the Rams didn't know what we were going to do. The trouble was that we didn't know either."

Most of the Baltimore plays were sent in by the coach, Don Shula. But one time, when Matte was out of bounds in front of the Colts bench, Shula gave Matte the next play directly. When Tom just looked at him, Shula repeated the instructions twice, each time louder.

"Don't you hear me, Tom?" the coach bellowed.

"Sure, but so does the entire Ram team."

But the strategy—and taped "crib sheet" —worked. Early in the fourth quarter, the Rams led, 17–10, but Matte drove the Colts eighty-five yards to a touchdown in a thirteen-play drive and then set up the deciding field goal. The Colts kept their playoff hopes alive by winning, 20–17.

In a way, they had their victory on tape.

Hot Dog!

Only days before, kick-returner Bob Gladieux had been cut by the New England Patriots, but here he was in the stands to watch the team play the Redskins in the opening game of the 1970 season. Bob had just told his friends he was going for a hot dog, when he heard his name being called over the public address system.

Next thing his friends knew, Gladieux was in uniform and about to return the opening kickoff. Patriots coach Clive Rush had cut two players just before game time and was short a kick-returner so he invited Bob back to play, and apparently Bob was glad to help.

Fowl Play

It almost became an international incident.

On a warm, foggy night in July 1983, seagulls flew slowly above the field at Toronto's Exhibition Stadium and several came to rest on the outfield turf.

In the middle of the fifth inning of the baseball game that night between the New York Yankees and Toronto Blue Jays, the Yankee outfielders had finished their warm-up tosses. Outfielder Dave Winfield took the extra ball they'd been throwing around and tossed it toward the ballboy near the New York bullpen. The ball took one hop and struck one of the gulls that had landed in the outfield, killing it.

As the bird's remains were removed, Winfield put his cap over his heart, a gesture that didn't sit well with the bird-loving Blue Jay fans, who tossed debris on the field and chanted insults. Considered special, the seagull was a protected species in Canada.

The matter didn't end there. At the conclusion of the game, Winfield was arrested by a plainclothes policeman, who advised him of his rights and charged him with cruelty to animals under a section of the Canadian Criminal Code that made "causing unnecessary suffering to any animal" a crime. It was punishable by up to a $500 fine and six months in jail. The police took Dave to a stationhouse, where he posted a bond and signed autographs.

Before the date Winfield was to appear to answer charges, a senior Crown attorney announced he'd request the charges against the ballplayer be dropped. Dave said he felt badly about the incident, which he said "the Toronto police realize...was an accident."

Take Me Out to the Ball *Pork*

Instead of having a ball boy or girl deliver baseballs to the home plate umpire, the St. Paul Saints of the independent Northern league have a ball *pig*. To the delight of the crowd, the swine hams it up by delivering new baseballs carried in a saddle bag slung over its piggy back.

The pig wears different outfits—such as a tutu or a bunny tail—and, on Opening Day, is dressed in a tuxedo. For a St. Patrick's Day promotion, the pig is painted green.

But the Saints' pig doesn't hog *all* the honors. The team does have bat boys and, in the outfield, ball girls. But when it comes to bringing home the bacon—delivering the balls to the home plate umpire—the responsibility is exclusively the pig's.

Cap Trick

Here's a play designed to cap-ture the hearts of baseball fans.

When Smokey Burgess hit a line drive to left center, outfielder Wally Moon grabbed the ball. Just as he released his throw to the infield, his cap flipped off his head and, amazingly, the ball hit the cap while it was sailing in the air. Burgess got an extra-base hit, and Moon was charged with an error.

"I'll bet I couldn't hit that cap again if I made a million throws," Moon said. "But that's baseball, filled with the impossible."

Saints Alive

Many sports figures believe in the power of prayer. Just watch a hitter before he steps into the batter's box, or, when he's not jumping around, a football player after he's scored a touchdown.

For instance, Herb Score, an ace pitcher for the Cleveland Indians, (whose career ended when he was hit in the eye by a line drive) said when he faced a tough situation on the mound, he prayed to St. Jude, the saint of impossible causes. The trouble was, Herb added, the batter prayed to him too.

A Rock and a Hard Place

After Tiger Woods teed off on the 13th hole in the final round of the 1999 Phoenix Open gold tournament, he found himself between a rock and a hard place. His ball had landed directly in front of a 1,000-pound boulder. There was no room for him to take a good swing, so at his request a dozen fans lifted the boulder out of the way (which was legal, since it wasn't stuck in the ground).

Tiger continued playing and birdied the hole (making it in one stroke under par).

CHAPTER

7

NOT MY JOB

Sometimes athletes get into game situations in which they fulfill roles they really weren't trained for. Here are a few...

Don't Throw, Garo

Football players usually have very specific roles to play on a team, and it's best that they stick to their assigned tasks. Some are supposed to just defend, others to block, yet others to return kicks, and so on. But there are times...

For instance, in the Super Bowl played in January 1973, between the Miami Dolphins and the Washington Redskins, Miami was at the Redskins' forty-two-yard line. With just over two minutes left in the game, Miami led, 14–0. Deciding to try for a field goal, the Dolphins sent in Garo Yapremian, their slight, baldish, Cyprus-born specialist, who kicked soccer style.

The snap from center was low, forcing the holder, Earl Morrall, to position the ball in a hurry. Still, Garo managed to hit the ball well, but it didn't get up in the air quickly enough and the Redskins managed to break through and block the kick.

Garo recovered the ball, but didn't think fast enough, and instead of falling on it as he should have, tried a pass. The Redskins' Mike Bass intercepted the ball and, despite Garo's futile attempt to tackle him, ran forty-nine yards for a touchdown, Washington's first score. The 'Skins were now within one touchdown of tying the game.

"My mind went blank," said Garo, explaining his attempt to throw a pass. "I just saw some uniforms downfield. I don't know who they were. But the ball slipped out of my hand."

Garo, who kicked lefty but threw righty, said his only experience throwing passes was in practice "when I throw to the guys just for fun. This wasn't fun." Luckily for Garo, the Dolphins held on to win, 14–7, for an unbeaten season.

Masked Man

In the closing seconds of a hockey game, the trailing team will often try a desperation tactic: lifting its goalie for another skater. The stratagem gives the team one more potential scorer, but also leaves its net undefended.

With 44.6 seconds left in the first game of the 1996–97 playoffs between the New Jersey Devils and Montreal Canadiens, and the Devils ahead, 4–2, the Canadiens pulled their goalie and replaced him with a shooter.

But Martin Brodeur of the Devils, at the

side of his own net, got the puck and lofted it high in the air. The puck sailed and slid 178 feet down the ice and into the undefended Canadien goal, making the score, 5–2.

What made the long shot remarkable was the fact the shooter was the Devils goalie! With this goal, Brodeur became only the second goaltender in NHL history to score a playoff goal (the other was Ron Hextall of the Philadelphia Flyers, who scored against the Washington Capitals on April 11, 1989).

Brodeur, who often would shoot the puck over opponents when killing penalties, had practiced that shot two or three times a week, and had been talking for years about some day scoring. "I was going for it, for sure," he said, adding "At least five times in my career, I've had better chances. And this one went in."

When he scored at last, he called it "the greatest thing that has happened to me personally...I freaked out. When I shot it, everyone was in my way and I lost [sight of] it...I finally saw it the last fifteen feet. I will never forget that moment. It was due to happen one of these days. I try it so much. I take a lot of pride in playing the puck."

Anywhere, Anytime

Two Major League baseball players played all nine positions in a single game (playing an inning at each position). Bert Campaneris did it for Kansas City on September 8, 1965, and Cesar Tovar did it for Minnesota on September 22, 1968.

Hot Bobsledders

The island of Jamaica is tropical and never has snow. Yet, as strange as it seems, Jamaica fielded a four-man bobsled team at the 1988 Olympic Games in Calgary, Canada.

The Jamaican bobsledders had never seen snow or trained on a real bobsled run, until just a few months before the Games. Using a bobsled with wheels, they had trained on a concrete slope. When it got to the Games, the team couldn't finish its run, crashing along the way.

However, their reggae theme song, "Hobbin' and a Bobbin'," was successful and they were the subject of a movie, *Cool Runnings*, starring John Candy and Doug E. Doug.

What a Week

Besides possibly Bo Jackson, no one in the modern era has played in two professional sports as effectively and dramatically as Deion Sanders.

On September 5, 1989, playing at Seattle, he hit a homer for the New York Yankees. Then five days later, having taken off Yankee pinstripes for football pads and helmet, Deion made his NFL debut as cornerback for the Atlanta Falcons.

Deion arrived late for the Falcons' September 10 game against the Los Angeles Rams, but got into the contest in the first quarter. Deion waved his arms and led the crowd in cheers as he awaited a punt. He momentarily fumbled the ball, but quickly recovered on his own 32-yard line, where he took two hits, circled back to the Atlanta 20 and then, although hit three more times, broke loose for a 68-yard touchdown run.

Deion thus became the only professional athlete in modern history to hit a major league home run and score an NFL touchdown in the same week!

CHAPTER
8

UNUSUAL INJURIES

The nature of the games that athletes play is such that they're constantly subject to injury. But sometimes, injuries come not from crushing blocks or tackles, wildly thrown balls, collisions and the like, but from odd, unexpected situations.

Picture This

It was a Kodak moment that, to be candid, turned negative.

"Iron Man" Cal Ripken Jr. of the Baltimore Orioles had played in more games in a row—without missing a single one—than any other player in Major League baseball history.

Coming into the 1996 All-Star game, his streak was at 2,239 consecutive games over fifteen seasons. Cal had been drilled by pitched fastballs and been slid into by runners trying to break up double plays; he'd had colds and aches and pains, but fortunately, in all that time, in all those games, he'd never suffered a broken bone.

Then, while posing for the American League team photograph before the 1996 All-Star Game in Philadelphia, the player standing next to him, pitcher Roberto Hernandez, lost his balance. Trying to keep from falling off the platform, Roberto threw back his arm and unintentionally whacked Cal in the nose, breaking it and knocking it out of place.

Nervous and panicky, Roberto offered Cal his shirt to help stop the bleeding and popped back the nose his forearm had displaced. Two teammates kiddingly offered to get Hernandez a bodyguard next time he played in Baltimore against Ripken's team.

Cal told reporters: "The first thing I had in my mind was to keep this a secret because the last thing I wanted to do is go down in All-Star history as the only guy to get injured in the team picture."

Would the freak accident end Ripken's streak?

Luckily, it would take more than a broken nose to stop the Iron Man. With gauze stuffed in his nose to stop the gushing blood, Cal took infield practice, then played in the game. And when the regular season resumed, he kept playing without missing a game.

Happily for all of baseball, the American League team picture wasn't a photo finish for his streak, which ultimately lasted 2,632 games.

Shock Jock

As a twenty-year-old apprentice plumber, future Olympic kayaker Cliff Meidl was actually electrocuted (!) when a jackhammer he was operating hit three live electric cables. For thirty seconds, thirty thousand volts of electricity shot through him. As a result of the incident he suffered three cardiac arrests, had two toes blown off, a third of his knee joints were burned, and one of his shoulder blades exploded. He faced possible leg amputation. He was ready to give up hope.

But after months in a hospital and in a wheelchair and two years on crutches, he started rowing a canoe as part of his therapy, and went on to become a great canoeist and then kayaker.

Cliff might not have discovered kayaking if not for his accident. He has maintained a sense of humor about the electrocution, enjoying jokes about his "shocking" experience.

Tough Town

When Clive Rush first joined the New England Patriots (from the New York Jets) as head coach in 1969, he was about to make the customary remarks about how pleased he was to be with his new club. He grasped a microphone and let out a scream—a faulty microphone plug gave him a severe electric shock. After someone pulled the plug out of the socket and Rush was revived, he said: "I knew the Boston media was going to be tough, but this is ridiculous."

Bad Breaking Pitch

Fastball pitcher Jake Slaughter of the Zion Hill Billies had a 3–0 lead over the Webb Farmers in the sixth inning of a game August 3, 1939 in Medina, Tennessee.

Getting ready to throw his blazing fastball, Jake broke his pitching arm by banging it against his forehead.

The game had to be stopped because of the fluke injury—Jake was the only pitcher for his team.

Tarp Trouble

Rain indirectly caused an injury to Cardinal outfielder Vince Coleman during the 1985 National League playoffs. When it started to rain before game 4 in St. Louis, the mechanical tarpaulin (the covering used to protect the infield from the weather) started rolling. Vince, not paying attention, got caught under the tarp, and was so severely bruised he had to sit out the remainder of the playoffs.

De-Fence!

It was beyond the *wall* of duty.

Rodney McCray, an outfielder for the Vancouver Canadians, was so intent on catching a fly ball in a minor league game in Portland, Oregon in May 1991, that he slammed right through the wooden fence.

Wacky Swinger

Putt yourself in his place.

Many an athlete will do whatever it takes to win, but golfer Lee Petters may have carried it a step too far.

In February 1997, Petters was playing in the Asian Hondo Classic in Bangna, Thailand, his first tournament as a full-time professional. Lee walked off the 14th tee, right into the club being practice-swung by his partner, Shakeep Hussain of Pakistan.

The club whacked Petters in the nose, splitting it open and sending him to the ground for several minutes. Three towels were needed to absorb the blood that was pouring from the wound.

The blow may have wiped (out) his nose, but Petters recovered well enough to get up and resume playing. Because he birdied the next hole (meaning he sank the ball in one stroke less than par), "I told him to hit me again."

His partner didn't oblige, but Petters had a good enough day to take the lead in the tournament temporarily, with a six-under-par 66. Who "nose" how well he might have done if he *had* been whacked again?

Tempting Targets

Ron Hunt of the Montreal Expos was hit by a pitch fifty times in 1971 and a total of 243 times in his lifetime. But American Leaguer Don Baylor (who from 1970 to 1988, played for Baltimore, Oakland, California, New York, Boston and Minnesota) holds the record of being hit by a pitch 267 times.

Dive Right In

Maybe John Maxon, professional high diver, doesn't want to make waves. Asked about diving from heights up to eighty feet, he said: "It's the safest thing in the world. But it could kill you."

9

PRACTICAL AND NOT-SO-PRACTICAL JOKES

Some athletes, no matter how good they were on the playing field, court or rink, were also stars at practical joking.

An Eggs-elent Prank

Usually in football, it's the quarterback who scrambles. Here's a case of a scrambling kicker. No *yoking!*

Horst Muhlmann, a former professional soccer player who was a place kicker for the Philadelphia Eagles in the mid-1970s, was very particular about caring for his football helmet. So much so that, even though the distance between the team's training camp locker room and practice field was only about half a mile, Horst would drive over and be certain to keep his helmet upright on the passenger seat.

One Sunday afternoon, three of his team-mates (Jerry Sisemore, Guy Morriss and Tom Luken) asked trainer Otho Davis to help them get to the helmet so they could sabotage it. Using thin strips of tape, they hid a raw egg under a rubber piece at the top of the helmet, above the web suspension.

When Horst tried to put his helmet on, it didn't fit, so he began pushing it down on his head with both hands. Suddenly he heard a crack. It was the eggshell, but Horst thought it was his neck and let out a loud scream. Then egg began running down his face.

The *yolk* was on Horst, who was one shell-shocked player.

Something Fishy

In June 1969, two Seattle pitchers slipped into the Baltimore Oriole bullpen and put their benches on the roof. A few nights later, the Orioles avenged the deed by slipping into their opponents' bullpen and putting three goldfish into their water cooler.

The Scales of Justice

When Jim Bouton was a pitcher with the New York Yankees, he won a ham in a dollar raffle run by Mickey Mantle—only there was no ham.

To get back at him, Jim entered a fishing tournament organized by Mickey and won the weight competition with a ten-pound creature he'd bought in a store the day before. It remained a mystery as to why the big fish was the only one Bouton "caught." Not to mention that it was gray and just lay there cold as a mackerel while the fish caught by the others were green and lively.

Dissing the Stanley Cup

The revered Stanley Cup—for which National Hockey League teams play their hearts out, and for a glimpse of which fans stand in line for hours—doesn't always receive respectful treatment after it's been won and taken home overnight by the team captain and other winning players.

For instance, once during the three-year reign of the Ottawa Silver Seven, one of the celebrating players responded to a challenge and kicked the Cup into the Rideau Canal near Ottawa. The next morning, the players came back to look for the prized trophy and were relieved to find the Cup dented but intact on the solidly frozen canal.

In July 1994, after the New York Rangers won the Cup, they did some horsing around with it. Left wing Eddie Olczyk, an admirer of thoroughbred horses, arranged to have the Cup brought out to Belmont Racetrack, to be displayed in the winner's circle. But somehow a Kentucky Derby-winning horse named Go for Gin ended up using the Cup as a water bucket.

CHAPTER
10

KNOCK WOOD, I'M NOT SUPERSTITIOUS

Many a player, coach or manager believes that a certain object or pattern behavior brings good luck in a game—or at least prevents bad luck. And who can say they're wrong?

For instance, Rudy Tomjanovich, coach of the Houston Rockets, drives to the arena by the same route each game and leaves courtside at the same time prior to the tip-off (at 6:37 for a 7:30 game). Mark Jackson of the Indiana Pacers plays with his wedding band tied on his sneaker laces. Kevin Duckworth, who played for the L.A. Clippers, put his left sock and shoe on first, ever since fifth grade. Trevor Ruffin used to wear two different pairs of socks when playing.

Getting Over Mike Fright

One of the most superstitious baseball players of all time was pitcher Mike Cuellar, who'd sit on the "lucky" end of the training bench, wear gold medallions, avoid the the top dugout step and, of course, refuse to step on a foul line.

In 1972 when Mike was with the Baltimore Orioles, only Jim Frey could warm him up and only Elrod Hendricks could pretend to be the batter. In between innings, Mike would not warm up with a substitute catcher, but insisted that the game catcher take his throws.

Mike, who also pitched for Houston, among others, would never take the mound until all his teammates were at their positions. And when he took his position, the ball had to be waiting for him at the mound, not thrown to him.

One time, Alex Johnson, who made the final out of an inning, picked up the ball and waited for him. Cuellar, who'd come out to warm up, refused to take the ball from Alex, who, in turn, refused to toss it on the ground. So Mike pretended to be paying attention to something else, while Johnson followed him and tried to force the ball on him, but Cuellar remained adamant.

But how could you argue with Cuellar about his superstitions? They seemed to work for him. Mike was co-winner of the Cy Young Award in 1969 and once struck out *four* men in a single inning.

The Same Old Drill

Bill Parcells, a legendary figure who retired from coaching after the 1999 football season, had a Tuesday dentist appointment three weeks in a row. Each of those weeks, his team won. So on the fourth Tuesday, there he was in the dentist's chair again, even though he didn't need anything done!

Who's Afraid of Number 13?

Some athletes deliberately choose to wear number 13 on their uniforms. Among NBA players: Kendall Gill of the New Jersey Nets, Mark Jackson of the Indiana Pacers, Luc Longley of the Phoenix Suns, Glenn Robinson of the Milwaukee Bucks,

Todd Day of the Miami Heat and Doug Christie of the Toronto Raptors. Wilt Chamberlain wore number 13 when he played with the Lakers and 76ers.

But the Atlanta Braves were not so brave. In 1978, by executive decree, they banned number 13 throughout their major and minor league system.

Designated Sitter

You've heard of the Designated Hitter, of course, but what about Designated *Bench Sitter?*

John McGraw, who was manager of the New York Giants from 1902 to 1932, kept Charles Victory Faust on the roster and had him sit on the bench in uniform because he thought the non-player brought the team good luck.

McGraw kept telling Faust he would get to pitch—and he finally did, for one inning.

With their designated good-luck charm on the bench, the Giants won three pennants in a row, 1911, 1912, and 1913. They lost the pennant in 1914. Charles Victory Faust had died before the season began.

They "Dig" the Message

As defensive coordinator for the New England Patriots, Al Groh would plant a rusty old shovel behind the bench at games, to remind the players to dig in and hustle.

He started the custom after a loss on November 6, 1994, and then the Patriots won their final seven games of the season.

"You're tired in the last quarter," said lineback Chris Slade. "You look over and see the shovel. You've got to find a way to dig deep."

Confidence Was the Mane Thing

Some old-time baseball players believed seeing white horses on the day of the game would bring good luck. One day in 1901, Frank Bowerman, the New York Giants catcher, told his manager, Hall of Famer John McGraw, that he'd noticed a team of white horses driving past the Polo Grounds. "That's a good sign," Frank said. "Watch me kill the ball this afternoon."

With new confidence, he did just that. The next day, another player saw the white horses, and so it went. "Funny how those white horses always happen to drive past the ballpark just when we are coming into the clubhouse," said one of the players. "It's certainly lucky."

The manager (known as "Little Napoleon" to sportswriters and "Mr. McGraw" to his players) just smiled. He'd hired the driver and horses the day that Bowerman first noticed them.

Pluck for Luck

Wade Boggs, one of the great pure hitters in baseball history, is also considered one of its most superstitious players as well.

Seemingly obsessed with the numbers 7 and 17, he signed a contract for $717,000 in 1984.

He was obviously a plucky player. Before a game, he'd adhere to an unvarying schedule and always dine on chicken, in one of fifty varieties prepared by his wife, Debbie. At the other kind of plate, home plate, he'd draw a *chai*, the Hebrew number 18, which symbolizes "life."

The Gospel Truth

From 1983 to 1994, when they faced an important game, the Minnesota Vikings made sure to have gospel singer Tom Tipton perform the national anthem. In games at which Tom sang "The Star-Spangled Banner," the Vikings were 11–0. But then they lost the next two games at which he sang, ruining the lucky streak.

They've Got His Number

Larry Walker, slugger with the Expos and then the Rockies, has a "thing" for the number 3.

On the Expos, he wore number 33, because another player was already wearing number 3, and he wore 33 with the Rockies. Larry was married on November 3, 1990, at 3:33 p.m. He'd always take the third locker from a corner in a locker room, take three practice swings and, when there are three doors from which to choose for entering a building, he chooses the third from the left.

Chance Took No Chances

In the days when baseball teams traveled by train, Frank Chance, the well-known infielder with the Chicago Cubs, would sleep only in bunk number 13. Frank took no chances; if that number was unavailable, he'd take another bunk and paint a number 13 on it.

Same Old Routine

Mike Hargrove used to walk up the first baseline and take three practice swings, then at the plate he'd dig a hole with his left foot, adjust the batting glove on his right hand, and wipe sweat off his upper lip with the crook of his left elbow. He'd pull one shoulder of his uniform, push down on his batting helmet and pull up his pants.

He'd then be ready to bat. But if the pitcher stepped off the rubber, Mike, who played for the San Diego Padres, Cleveland Indians and Texas Rangers, would repeat the routine.

Staving Off Defeat

In the early 1900s, many baseball players thought seeing a wagonload of barrels before a game meant good luck. Jake Ruppert, owner of the Yankees, would sometimes hire a wagon to circle Yankee Stadium before games.

Here's the Dirt

When he managed the San Francisco Giants, Roger Craig kept a jar of dirt on his desk from the infield of the Iowa cornfield where *Field of Dreams* was filmed. The dirt had been sent to him by a fan. The Giants enjoyed a nine-game winning streak and, said Craig, "I made sure that jar of dirt didn't disappear."

Despite Craig taking the jar on the road with him, his team lost on a no-hitter by Terry Mulholland of the Philadelphia Phillies.

But there was a good deal of superstition on the part of the other team as well. Darren Daulton, who was Mulholland's catcher that night, didn't want to do anything that might jeopardize the no-hitter. So, even though it was a hot, humid night, and he ordinarily would have changed mitts midway through the game, he kept wearing the same mitt, though the inside was perspiration-soaked. "I would never have forgiven myself if I changed mitts, and then he lost the no-hitter." Daulton suffered with a soggy glove, and Mulholland made his way into the history books—and into this book too!